Contents

About
Writing Centers
Grades 2-3

What's Great About This Book

Centers are a wonderful, fun way for students to practice important skills. The 13 centers in this book are self-contained and portable. Students may work at a desk, at a table, or even on the floor. Once you've made the centers, they're ready to use any time.

What's in This Book

The teacher directions page includes how to make the center and a description of the student task

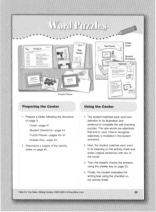

Full-color materials needed for the center

Reproducible activity sheets to practice and evaluate writing skills

Portfolio cover and student center checklist

How to Use the Centers

The centers are intended for skill practice, not to introduce skills. It is important to model the use of each center before students do the task independently.

Questions to Consider:

- Will students select a center, or will you assign the centers?
- Will there be a specific block of time for centers, or will the centers be used throughout the day?
- Where will you place the centers for easy access by students?
- What procedure will students use when they need help with the center tasks?
- How will you track the tasks and centers completed by each student?

Making a File Folder Center

Folder centers are easily stored in a box or file crate. Students take a folder to their desks to complete the task.

Materials:

- folder with pockets
- envelopes
- marking pens and pencils
- scissors
- stapler
- two-sided tape

Folder Back

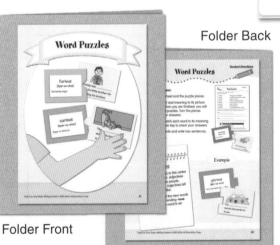

Folder Front

Steps to Follow:

1. Laminate the cover. Tape it to the front of the folder.

2. Laminate the student directions page. Tape it to the back of the folder.

3. Place activity sheets, writing paper, and any other supplies in the left-hand pocket.

4. Laminate the task cards. Place each set of task cards in an envelope. Place the labeled envelopes in the right-hand pocket.

5. If needed for the center, laminate the sorting mat and place it in the right-hand pocket of the folder.

6. If needed for the center, laminate and assemble the self-checking answer key pages into a booklet. Place them in the left-hand pocket of the folder.

Student Portfolio

If desired, make a writing portfolio for each student. Reproduce pages 5 and 6 for each student. Attach the cover to the front of a file folder. Attach the student center checklist to the inside front cover of the folder. Place the portfolio folders in an area accessible to both students and teacher.

Center Checklist

Student Names

Centers

Draw and Write: Forest Animals										
On the Move										
Word Puzzles										
Make a Complete Sentence										
Shape Poem										
Parts of a Story										
Exciting Words										
Eight on a List										
Vacation Postcards										
Story Starters										
A Friendly Letter										
Checking for Errors										
How Do You Do It?										

Take It to Your Seat—Writing Centers • EMC 6003 • © Evan-Moor Corp.

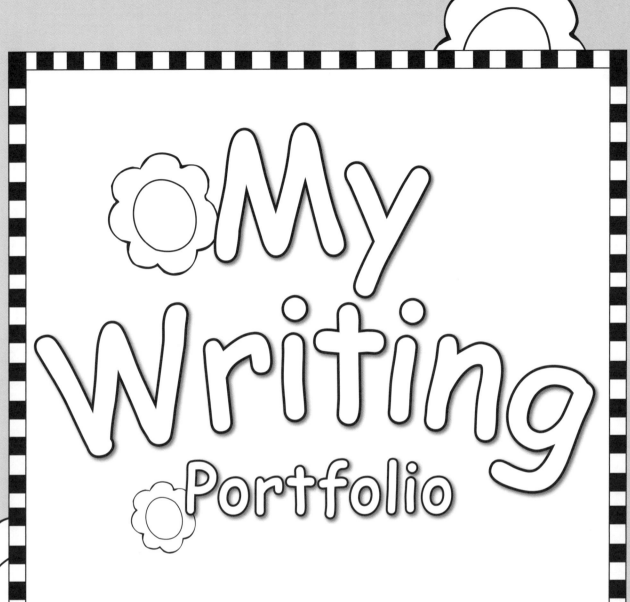

My Writing Portfolio

_____

Name

Writing Centers Checklist

Name _____

Check the writing centers that you have completed.

❏ Draw and Write: Forest Animals

❏ On the Move

❏ Word Puzzles

❏ Make a Complete Sentence

❏ Shape Poem

❏ Parts of a Story

❏ Exciting Words

❏ Eight on a List

❏ Vacation Postcards

❏ Story Starters

❏ A Friendly Letter

❏ Checking for Errors

❏ How Do You Do It?

Draw and Write:
Forest Animals

Task Cards

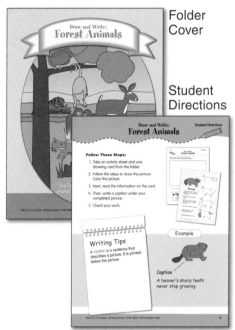

Folder Cover

Student Directions

Preparing the Center

1. Prepare a folder following the directions on page 3.

    Cover—page 9

    Student Directions—page 11

    Task Cards—pages 13–23

2. Reproduce a supply of the activity sheet on page 8.

Using the Center

1. The student selects a task card and an activity sheet.

2. The student follows the drawing steps to draw the picture described on the card. The student is encouraged to color the completed picture.

3. Next, the student uses the information on the card to write a caption below the final picture. How to write a caption is modeled in the student directions.

4. Finally, the student evaluates the writing task using the checklist on the activity sheet.

Draw and Write:
Forest Animals

Follow the steps on the card to draw the animal.
Color your picture. Write a caption about the animal.

_____

_____

✔ **Check Your Work**

○ I followed directions to draw an animal.

○ I wrote a caption that described the animal.

Draw and Write:
Forest Animals

The forest provides food and shelter for all kinds of animals.

Follow These Steps:

1. Take an activity sheet and one drawing card from the folder.

2. Follow the steps to draw the picture. Color the picture.

3. Next, read the information on the card.

4. Then, write a caption under your completed picture.

5. Check your work.

Writing Tips

A caption is a sentence that describes a picture. It is printed below the picture.

Example

Caption

A beaver's sharp teeth never stop growing.

12

White-Tailed Deer

Tan or brown with white on throat, around eyes and nose, and on stomach and underside of tail
Male deer called a "buck," has antlers
Fast runner—up to 30 miles an hour
Eats mostly grasses, flowers, buds, and young leaves
Female has one to three babies called "fawns"
Lives near the edge of forest

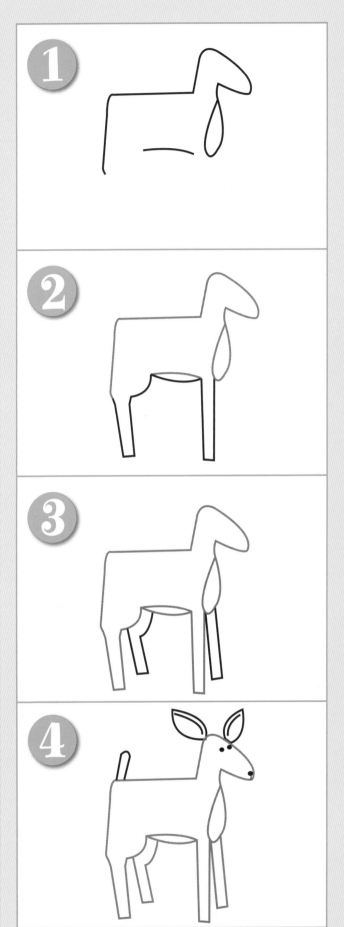

Draw and Write:
Forest Animals

© Evan-Moor Corp. • EMC 6003

Raccoon

Has black "mask" on face and black or brown rings on bushy tail
Front paws are used like hands
Eats fruit, nuts, bird eggs, and animals like crickets and mice
Is nocturnal (active at night)
Female has four to six babies called "kits"
Usually makes den in tree

Draw and Write:
Forest Animals

© Evan-Moor Corp. • EMC 6003

Beaver

Has thick brown fur and large flat tail
Can hold breath 10 to 15 minutes
Has sharp teeth that never stop growing
Eats tree bark, waterlily tubers, clover, fruit, and leaves
Female has three or four babies called "kits"
Builds lodge in water out of sticks and mud

Draw and Write:
Forest Animals

© Evan-Moor Corp. • EMC 6003

Gray Fox

Gray on top, reddish brown on sides and chest
Has pointed muzzle and long bushy tail
Eats fruit, nuts, berries, grass, and animals like insects, birds, mice, and rabbits
Only kind of fox that climbs trees
Female has one to seven babies called "pups"
Makes den in cave, hollow log, or hole in tree

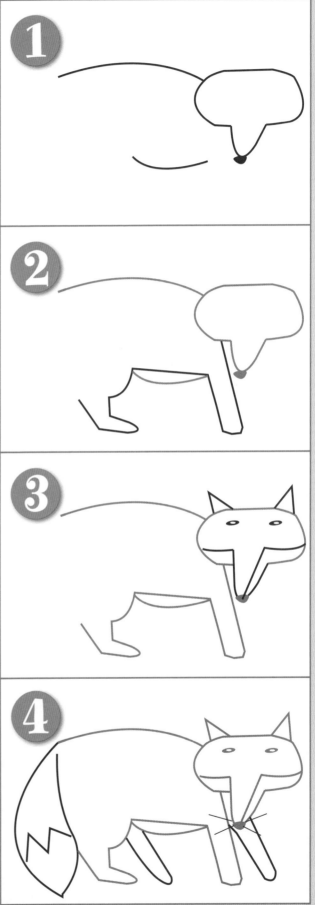

Draw and Write:
Forest Animals

© Evan-Moor Corp. • EMC 6003

Opossum

Only marsupial (animal that raises young in pouch) in North America
Eats almost anything (fruit, insects, small animals)
Nocturnal (active at night)
Plays "dead" when in danger
Female usually has seven or eight babies called "joeys," but may have up to 25 babies
Makes den in hollow tree or burrow in ground

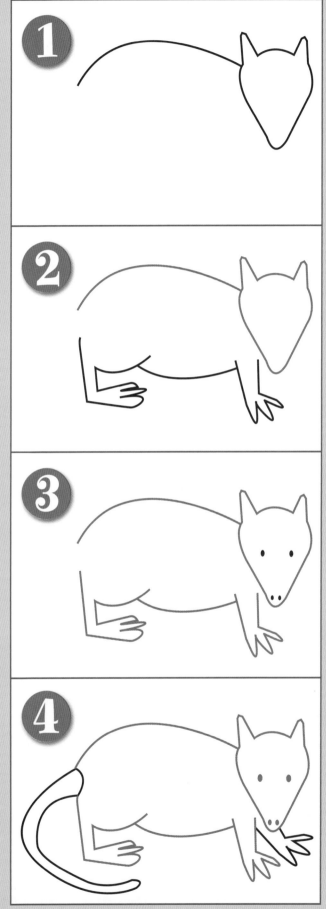

Draw and Write:
Forest Animals

© Evan-Moor Corp. • EMC 6003

Great Horned Owl

The largest owl in North America
Large tufts of feathers look like horns
Has very good eyesight and hearing
Hunts at night for small mammals and birds
Loosely-packed feathers make it almost silent when it flies
After eating, spits up bones and fur in owl pellets

Draw and Write:
Forest Animals

© Evan-Moor Corp. • EMC 6003

On the Move

Task Cards

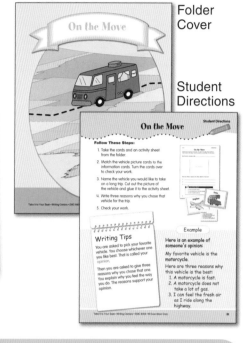

Folder Cover

Student Directions

Preparing the Center

1. Prepare a folder following the directions on page 3.

    Cover—page 29

    Student Directions—page 31

    Task Cards—pages 33–37

2. Reproduce a supply of the activity sheet on page 26 and the pictures on pages 27 and 28. Provide scissors and glue for student use.

Using the Center

1. The student takes the task cards and an activity sheet.

2. First, the student matches the pictures of the vehicles to the information cards. The cards are self-checking.

3. Next, the student chooses his or her favorite vehicle. The student cuts and glues the vehicle onto the activity sheet.

4. Then the student writes three reasons why the vehicle is the best. How to write an opinion and give supporting reasons is modeled in the student directions.

5. Finally, the student evaluates the writing task using the checklist on the activity sheet.

On the Move

Pretend you are going on a long trip. The route is from New York to California. That is almost 3,000 miles. Choose the vehicle you would take. Fill in the blanks.

My favorite vehicle is the _____ .

glue vehicle here

Here are three reasons why this vehicle is the best:

1. _____

2. _____

3. _____

✓ Check Your Work

◯ I chose my favorite vehicle.

◯ I wrote three reasons why I like the vehicle.

◯ I wrote complete sentences.

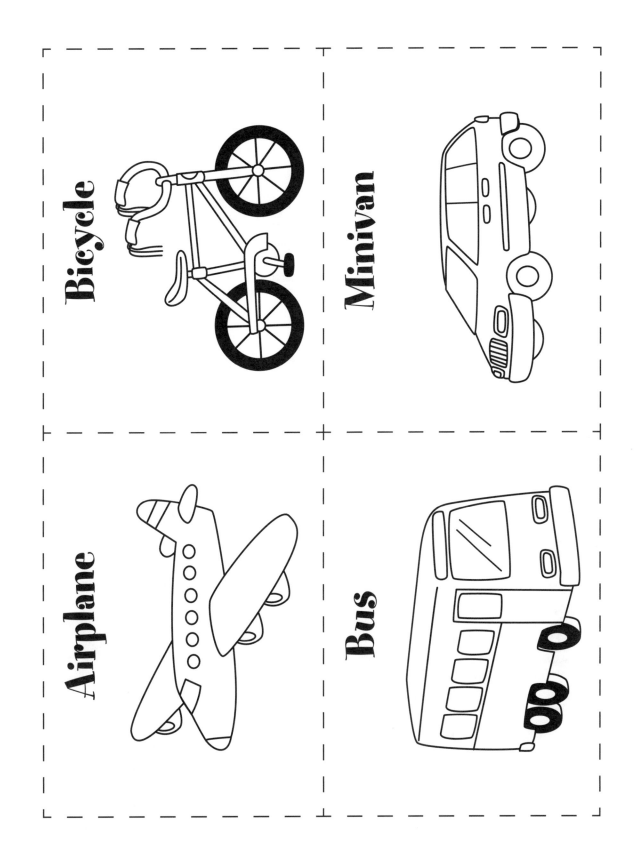

Bicycle

Minivan

Airplane

Bus

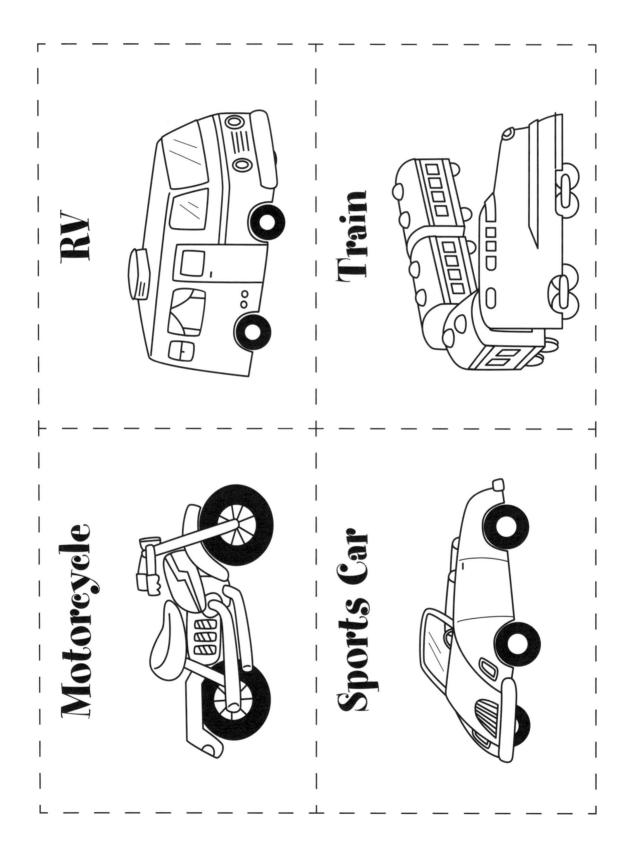

RV

Train

Motorcycle

Sports Car

On the Move

On the Move

Follow These Steps:

1. Take the cards and an activity sheet from the folder.

2. Match the vehicle picture cards to the information cards. Turn the cards over to check your work.

3. Name the vehicle you would like to take on a long trip. Cut out the picture of the vehicle and glue it to the activity sheet.

4. Write three reasons why you chose that vehicle for the trip.

5. Check your work.

Writing Tips

You are asked to pick your favorite vehicle. You choose whichever one you like best. That is called your opinion.

Then you are asked to give three reasons why you chose that one. You explain why you feel the way you do. The reasons support your opinion.

Example

Here is an example of someone's opinion:

My favorite vehicle is the **motorcycle.**

Here are three reasons why this vehicle is the best:
1. A motorcycle is fast.
2. A motorcycle does not take a lot of gas.
3. I can feel the fresh air as I ride along the highway.

Bicycle

Minivan

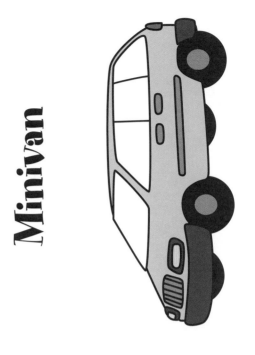

Airplane

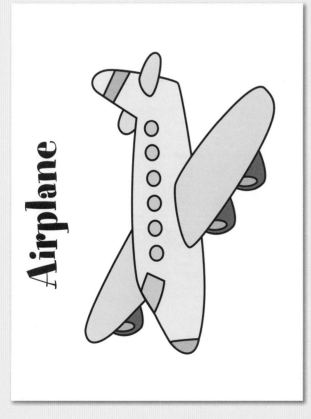

Bus

On the Move

On the Move

On the Move

On the Move

Motorcycle

RV

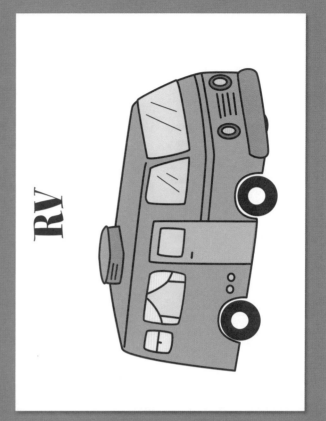

Sports Car

Train

On the Move

On the Move

On the Move

On the Move

This vehicle:
- is also called an **airliner**
- travels at 400 miles per hour
- has a pilot and copilot
- carries about 250 passengers

This vehicle:
- is also called a **road bike**
- can travel at 30 miles per hour
- has 1 rider
- carries 0 passengers

This vehicle:
- is also called an **intercity bus**
- travels at 65 miles per hour
- has 1 driver
- carries about 50 passengers

This vehicle:
- is also called a **van**
- travels at 65 miles per hour
- has 1 driver
- carries 7 to 9 passengers

This vehicle:
- is also called a **bike**
- travels at 65 miles per hour
- has 1 rider
- carries 1 passenger

This vehicle:
- is also called a **motor home**
- travels at 65 miles per hour
- has 1 driver
- most carry 2 to 10 passengers

This vehicle:
- is also called an **automobile**
- travels at 65 miles per hour
- has 1 driver
- most carry up to 4 passengers

This vehicle:
- is also called an **intercity train**
- most travel at about 130 miles per hour
- has an engineer who drives the train; the conductor helps passengers
- carries about 50 to 90 passengers

On the Move

On the Move

On the Move

On the Move

On the Move

On the Move

On the Move

On the Move

Word Puzzles

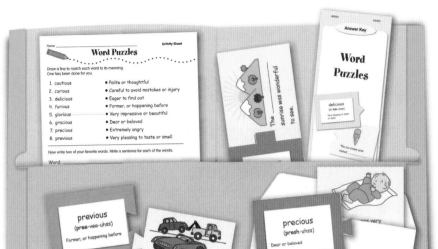

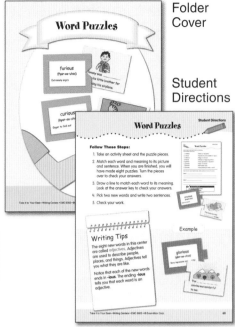

Folder Cover

Student Directions

Puzzle Pieces

Preparing the Center

1. Prepare a folder following the directions on page 3.

   Cover—page 41

   Student Directions—page 43

   Puzzle Pieces—pages 45–51

   Answer Key—page 53

2. Reproduce a supply of the activity sheet on page 40.

Using the Center

1. The student matches each word and definition to its illustration and sentence to complete the self-checking puzzles. The new words are adjectives that end in -ious. How to recognize adjectives is modeled in the student directions.

2. Next, the student matches each word to its meaning on the activity sheet and writes original sentences with two of the words.

3. Then the student checks the answers using the answer key on page 53.

4. Finally, the student evaluates the writing task using the checklist on the activity sheet.

Word Puzzles

Draw a line to match each word to its meaning.
One has been done for you.

1. cautious	● Polite or thoughtful
2. curious	● Careful to avoid mistakes or injury
3. delicious	● Eager to find out
4. furious	● Former, or happening before
5. glorious ————————	● Very impressive or beautiful
6. gracious	● Dear or beloved
7. precious	● Extremely angry
8. previous	● Very pleasing to taste or smell

Now write two of your favorite words. Write a sentence for each of the words.

Word: _____

_____

_____

Word: _____

_____

_____

✔ **Check Your Work**

◯ I used the new words correctly.

◯ I wrote complete sentences.

furious

(fyur-ee-uhss)

Extremely angry

Tommy was _____ his little brother for ...king his airplane.

curious

(kyur-ee-uhss)

Eager to find out

The ___ wa... to kno... cat in t...

Word Puzzles

Follow These Steps:

1. Take an activity sheet and the puzzle pieces.

2. Match each word and meaning to its picture and sentence. When you are finished, you will have made eight puzzles. Turn the pieces over to check your answers.

3. Draw a line to match each word to its meaning. Look at the answer key to check your answers.

4. Pick two new words and write two sentences.

5. Check your work.

Writing Tips

The eight new words in this center are called adjectives. Adjectives are used to describe people, places, and things. Adjectives tell you what they are like.

Notice that each of the new words ends in **-ious**. The ending **-ious** tells you that each word is an adjective.

Example

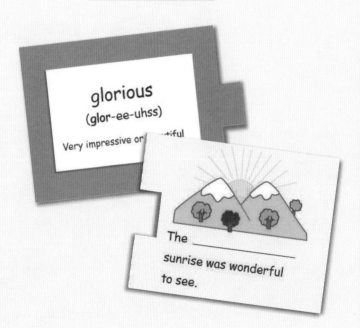

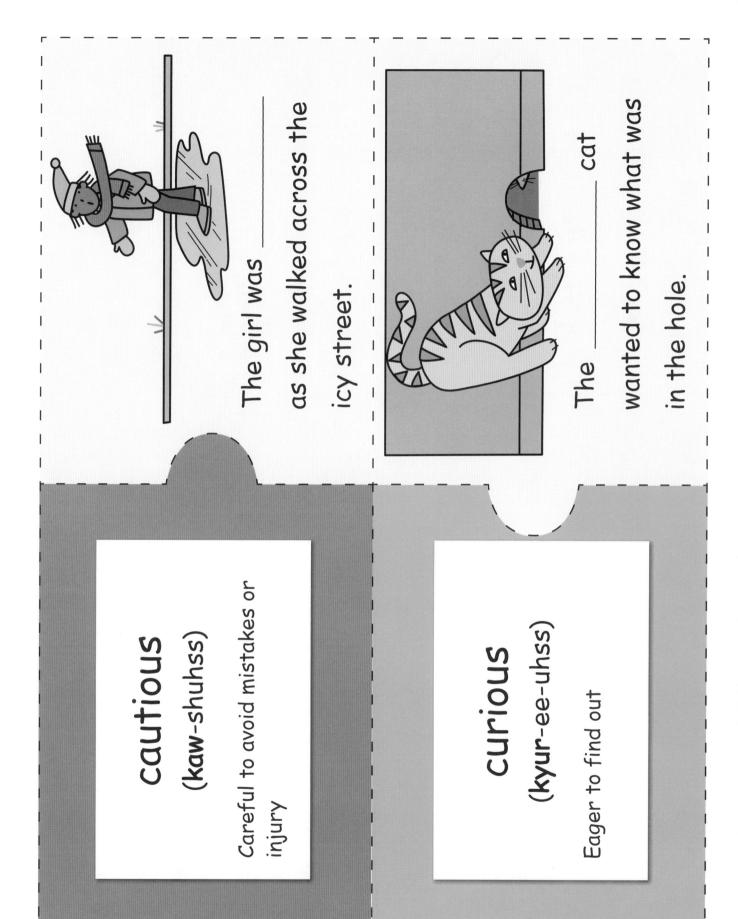

The girl was _____ as she walked across the icy street.

cautious
(**kaw**-shuhss)

Careful to avoid mistakes or injury

The _____ cat wanted to know what was in the hole.

curious
(**kyur**-ee-uhss)

Eager to find out

Word Puzzles

Word Puzzles

Word Puzzles

Word Puzzles

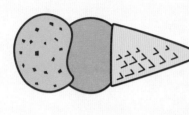

The ice-cream cone tasted _____.

Tommy was _____ with his little brother for breaking his airplane.

delicious
(di-**lish**-uhss)

Very pleasing to taste or smell

furious
(**fyur**-ee-uhss)

Extremely angry

Word Puzzles

© Evan-Moor Corp. • EMC 6003

Word Puzzles

© Evan-Moor Corp. • EMC 6003

Word Puzzles

© Evan-Moor Corp. • EMC 6003

Word Puzzles

© Evan-Moor Corp. • EMC 6003

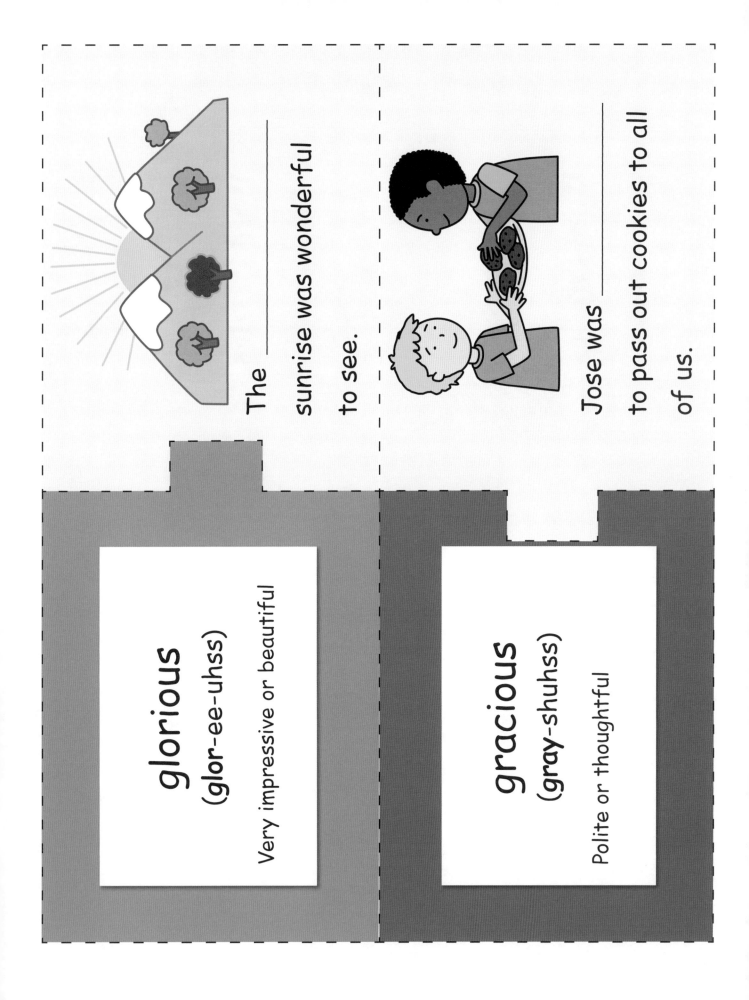

The _____ sunrise was wonderful to see.

Jose was _____ to pass out cookies to all of us.

glorious
(glor-ee-uhss)

Very impressive or beautiful

gracious
(gray-shuhss)

Polite or thoughtful

Word Puzzles

© Evan-Moor Corp. • EMC 6003

Word Puzzles

© Evan-Moor Corp. • EMC 6003

Word Puzzles

© Evan-Moor Corp. • EMC 6003

Word Puzzles

© Evan-Moor Corp. • EMC 6003

Their baby was very _____ to them.

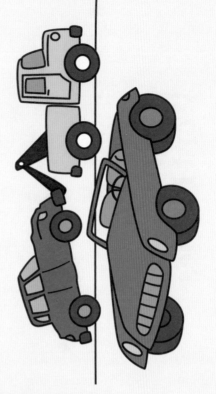

I like this new car more _____ than our _____ one.

precious (presh-uhss)

Dear or beloved

previous (pree-vee-uhss)

Former, or happening before

Word Puzzles

Word Puzzles

Word Puzzles

Word Puzzles

Word Puzzles

delicious
(di-**lish**-uhss)

Very pleasing to taste
or smell

The ice-cream cone
tasted _____ .

Lift the flap to check
your answers.

1. cautious — Careful to avoid mistakes or injury

2. curious — Eager to find out

3. delicious — Very pleasing to taste or smell

4. furious — Extremely angry

5. glorious — Very impressive or beautiful

6. gracious — Polite or thoughtful

7. precious — Dear or beloved

8. previous — Former, or happening before

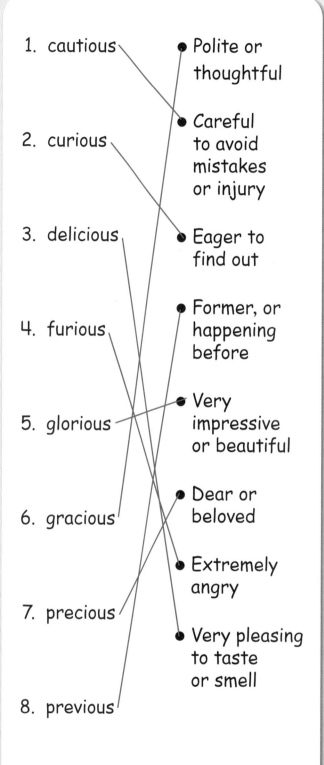

Polite or thoughtful

Careful to avoid mistakes or injury

Eager to find out

Former, or happening before

Very impressive or beautiful

Dear or beloved

Extremely angry

Very pleasing to taste or smell

Make a Complete Sentence

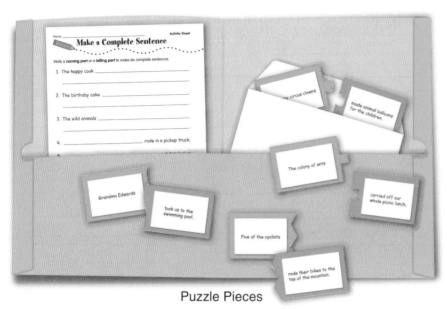

Puzzle Pieces

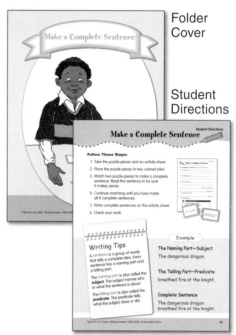

Folder Cover

Student Directions

Preparing the Center

1. Prepare a folder following the directions on page 3.

    Cover—page 57

    Student Directions—page 59

    Puzzle Pieces—pages 61 and 63

2. Reproduce a supply of the activity sheet on page 56.

Using the Center

1. The student sorts the puzzle pieces into two piles.

2. The student matches each subject and predicate puzzle piece to make a complete sentence. The student completes eight puzzles.

3. Then the student writes complete sentences on the activity sheet. How to recognize and write the two parts of a complete sentence is modeled in the student directions.

4. Finally, the student evaluates the writing task using the checklist on the activity sheet.

Make a Complete Sentence

Write a **naming part** or a **telling part** to make six complete sentences.

1. The happy cook _____

_____ .

2. The birthday cake _____

_____ .

3. The wild animals _____

_____ .

4. _____ rode in a pickup truck.

5. _____ got tangled up

in the ball of string.

6. _____ flipped off

the diving board.

✓ Check Your Work

- ◯ I made six complete sentences.
- ◯ The sentences I wrote make sense.
- ◯ I used interesting words.

Make a Complete Sentence

Make a Complete Sentence

Follow These Steps:

1. Take the puzzle pieces and an activity sheet.

2. Place the puzzle pieces in two colored piles.

3. Match two puzzle pieces to make a complete sentence. Read the sentence to be sure it makes sense.

4. Continue matching until you have made all 8 complete sentences.

5. Write complete sentences on the activity sheet.

6. Check your work.

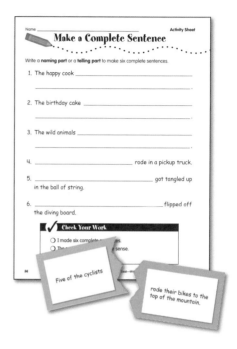

Writing Tips

A sentence is a group of words that tells a complete idea. Every sentence has a naming part and a telling part.

The naming part is also called the **subject**. The subject names who or what the sentence is about.

The telling part is also called the **predicate**. The predicate tells what the subject does or did.

Example

The Naming Part—Subject

The dangerous dragon

The Telling Part—Predicate

breathed fire at the knight.

Complete Sentence

The dangerous dragon breathed fire at the knight.

My pet snake Stan

slithered across the slippery floor.

The funny circus clowns

made animal balloons for the children.

Five of the cyclists

rode their bikes to the top of the mountain.

Popcorn and licorice

are my favorite movie snacks.

Make a Complete Sentence

Make a Complete Sentence

Make a Complete Sentence

Make a Complete Sentence

Make a Complete Sentence

Make a Complete Sentence

Make a Complete Sentence

Make a Complete Sentence

My big brother and I

like to play video games together.

The colony of ants

carried off our whole picnic lunch.

Grandma Edwards

took us to the swimming pool.

Our teacher Mr. Lee

does not give us homework on Fridays.

Make a Complete Sentence

Make a Complete Sentence

Make a Complete Sentence

Make a Complete Sentence

Make a Complete Sentence

Make a Complete Sentence

Make a Complete Sentence

Make a Complete Sentence

Shape Poem

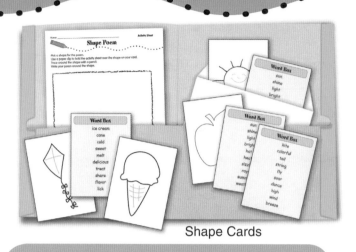

Shape Cards

Folder Cover

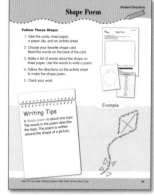

Student Directions

Preparing the Center

1. Prepare a folder following the directions on page 3.

   Cover—page 67

   Student Directions—page 69

   Shape Cards—pages 71–77

2. Reproduce a supply of the activity sheet on page 66. Provide a supply of lined paper and paper clips.

Using the Center

1. The student selects a shape card, an activity sheet, lined paper, and a paper clip.

2. First, the student makes a list of words and phrases about the topic. A word bank has been provided on the back of each card as a resource for the student.

3. Next, the student chooses the best words and phrases to use. The student arranges them to create a pleasing sound. How to write a shape poem is modeled in the student directions.

4. The student attaches the activity sheet to the shape card using a paper clip. The student traces around the shape.

5. Then the student writes the poem (words, phrases, or even sentences) around the shape.

6. Finally, the student evaluates the writing task using the checklist on the activity sheet.

Name _____

Shape Poem

Pick a shape for the poem.
Use a paper clip to hold the activity sheet over the shape on your card.
Trace around the shape with a pencil.
Write your poem around the shape.

✔ **Check Your Work**

◯ I planned which words to use.

◯ I wrote my poem around the shape.

Take It to Your Seat—Writing Centers • EMC 6003 • © Evan-Moor Corp.

Shape Poem

68

Shape Poem

Follow These Steps:

1. Take the cards, lined paper, a paper clip, and an activity sheet.

2. Choose your favorite shape card. Read the words on the back of the card.

3. Make a list of words about the shape on lined paper. Use the words to write a poem.

4. Follow the directions on the activity sheet to make the shape poem.

5. Check your work.

Writing Tips

A shape poem is about one topic. The words in the poem describe the topic. The poem is written around the shape of a picture.

Example

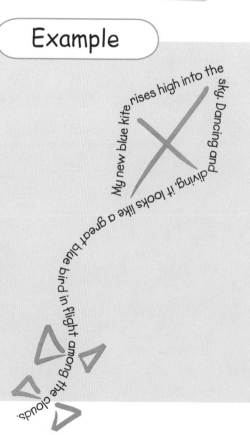

70

Word Box

sun
shine
light
bright
hot
heat
sizzle
rays
summer
weather

Word Box

apple
fruit
sweet
juicy
tasty
crunch
harvest
pick
snack
healthy

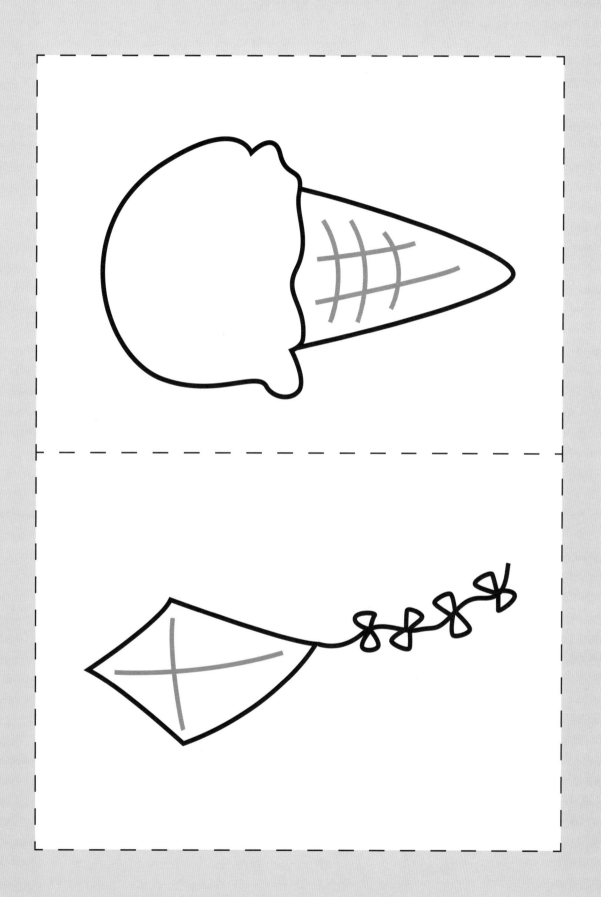

Word Box

ice cream

cone

cold

sweet

melt

delicious

treat

share

flavor

lick

Word Box

kite

colorful

tail

string

fly

soar

dance

high

wind

breeze

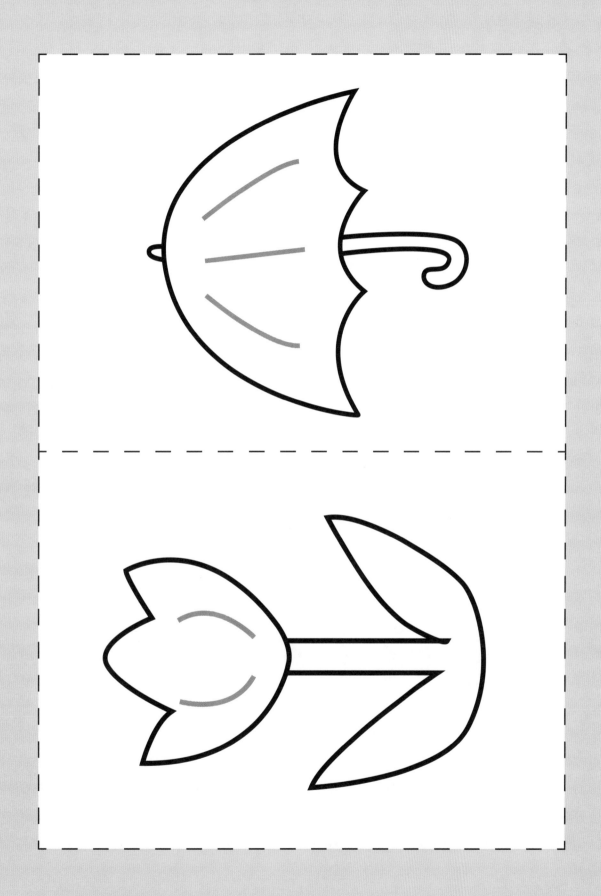

Word Box

umbrella

handle

open

unfurl

protect

cover

raindrops

puddles

plop

bounce

Word Box

tulip

flower

blossom

leaves

stem

bloom

grow

colorful

garden

spring

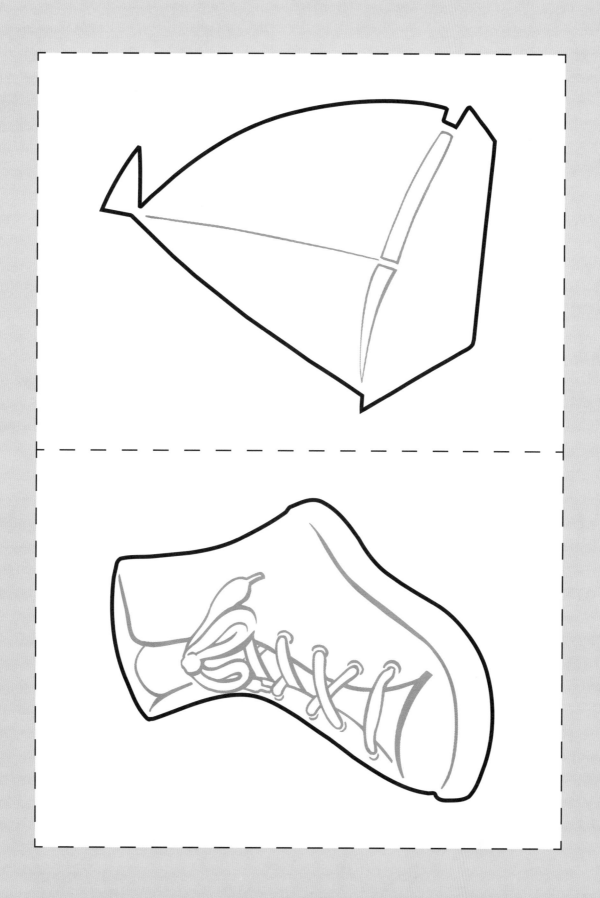

Word Box

sailboat

sails

wind

blow

float

bound

swift

waves

ocean

sea

Word Box

shoe

sneaker

laces

sole

feet

fit

race

leap

swift

hurry

Parts of a Story

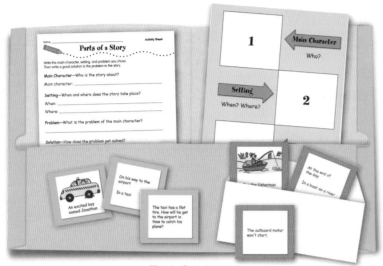

Task Cards

Folder Cover

Student Directions

Preparing the Center

1. Prepare a folder following the directions on page 3.

   Cover—page 81

   Student Directions—page 83

   Sorting Mat—page 85

   Task Cards—pages 87–95

2. Reproduce a supply of the activity sheet on page 80.

Using the Center

1. The student takes the task cards and an activity sheet from the folder. The student sorts the cards into sets by color.

2. Next, the student selects one set of three cards and places them on the sorting mat under the correct headings: Main Character, Setting, and Problem. The backs of the cards are self-checking. How to recognize the parts of a story is modeled in the student directions.

3. Then the student writes the three parts of the story on the activity sheet. The student uses the information to write a creative solution to the problem of the story.

4. Finally, the student evaluates the writing task using the checklist on the activity sheet.

Name _____

Parts of a Story

Write the main character, setting, and problem you chose.
Then write a good solution to the problem in the story.

Main Character—Who is the story about?

Main character: _____

Setting—When and where does the story take place?

When: _____

Where: _____

Problem—What is the problem of the main character?

_____

Solution—How does the problem get solved?

_____

_____

_____

Put this page in your writing portfolio.
Use the information to write a story another day.

✔ **Check Your Work**

◯ I chose a main character, a setting, and a problem.

◯ I wrote a good solution to the problem.

Parts of a Story

82

Parts of a Story

Follow These Steps:

1. Take the cards, the sorting mat, and an activity sheet.

2. Put the cards that are the same color together in sets.

3. Take one set of three cards. Put them in the correct squares on the sorting mat.

4. Write the main character, the setting, and the problem on the activity sheet.

5. Think of a way to solve the problem. Write your idea in the solution space.

6. Check your work.

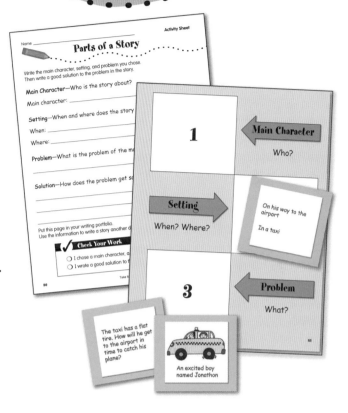

Writing Tips

When you plan a story, it is good to think about these four things:

1. **Who** is the story about? That is called the main character.

2. **When** and **where** is the story going to take place? That is called the setting.

3. **What** problem is the main character going to have? That is called the problem.

4. **How** is the problem going to get solved? That is called the solution.

Example

Main Character: a monkey

Setting: at night in a tropical rainforest

Problem: The monkey is hungry. He can't get the bananas because a snake is in the way.

Solution: The monkey will swing to another branch. He will eat bananas until he is full.

Take It to Your Seat—Writing Centers • EMC 6003 • © Evan-Moor Corp.

1

Main Character

Who?

Setting

When? Where?

2

3

Problem

What?

A white cat

A space alien

Early in the morning

At the back door

In the year 3000

Circling the Earth

The poor thing was left outside in the rain.

The spaceship is running out of fuel.

1

Parts of a Story

© Evan-Moor Corp. • EMC 6003

1

Parts of a Story

© Evan-Moor Corp. • EMC 6003

2

Parts of a Story

© Evan-Moor Corp. • EMC 6003

2

Parts of a Story

© Evan-Moor Corp. • EMC 6003

3

Parts of a Story

© Evan-Moor Corp. • EMC 6003

3

Parts of a Story

© Evan-Moor Corp. • EMC 6003

A talking parrot

Joe the fisherman

One afternoon

In the pet store

At the end of
the day

In a boat on a river

He won't come out
of his cage so the
family can buy him.

The outboard motor
won't start.

1

Parts of a Story

1

Parts of a Story

2

Parts of a Story

2

Parts of a Story

3

Parts of a Story

3

Parts of a Story

A frightened camper

An excited boy named Jonathon

At midnight

Inside the tent

On his way to the airport

In a taxi

She hears strange noises coming from the woods.

The taxi has a flat tire. How will he get to the airport in time to catch his plane?

1

Parts of a Story

1

Parts of a Story

2

Parts of a Story

2

Parts of a Story

3

Parts of a Story

3

Parts of a Story

A girl named Maria

A nervous jockey

On a hot summer day

At her lemonade stand

The day of the big race

At the fairgrounds

No one is stopping to buy her lemonade.

His racehorse is missing from the stall.

1

Parts of a Story

1

Parts of a Story

2

Parts of a Story

2

Parts of a Story

3

Parts of a Story

3

Parts of a Story

A worried acrobat

A confused usher

On Saturday

At the circus

During the movie

At the movie theater

The net below has a huge tear in it.

Popcorn is flying all over the theater.

1

Parts of a Story

1

Parts of a Story

2

Parts of a Story

2

Parts of a Story

3

Parts of a Story

3

Parts of a Story

Exciting Words

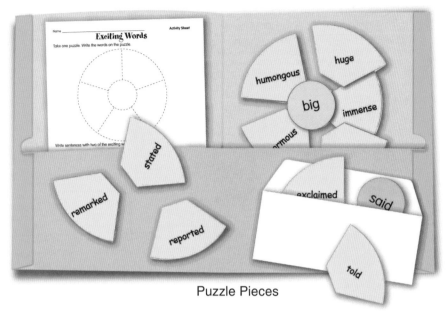

Puzzle Pieces

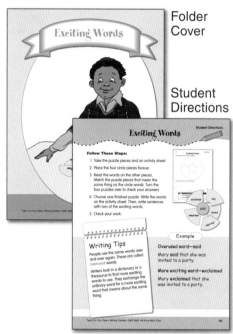

Folder Cover

Student Directions

Preparing the Center

1. Prepare a folder following the directions on page 3.

   Cover—page 99

   Student Directions—page 101

   Puzzle Pieces—pages 103–109

2. Reproduce a supply of the activity sheet on page 98.

Using the Center

1. The student takes the puzzle pieces and an activity sheet.

2. Next, the student looks for synonyms for the overused words on the circles, placing each word around the circle until all four puzzles are complete. How to replace overused words with more exciting words is modeled in the student directions.

3. Then the student selects one puzzle. The student writes the words on the activity sheet and writes sentences with two of the new words.

4. Finally, the student evaluates the writing task using the checklist on the activity sheet.

Exciting Words

Take one puzzle. Write the words on the puzzle.

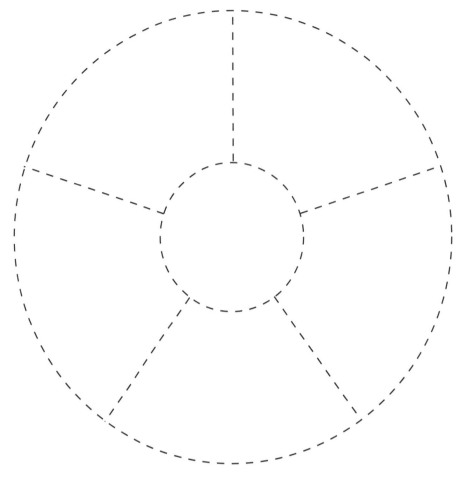

Write sentences with two of the exciting words.

1. _____

_____

2. _____

_____

 Check Your Work

⭕ I put the puzzle together correctly.

⭕ I wrote complete sentences.

Exciting Words

100

Exciting Words

Follow These Steps:

1. Take the puzzle pieces and an activity sheet.

2. Place the four circle pieces faceup.

3. Read the words on the other pieces. Match the puzzle pieces that mean the same thing as the circle words. Turn the four puzzles over to check your answers.

4. Choose one finished puzzle. Write the words on the activity sheet. Then, write sentences with two of the exciting words.

5. Check your work.

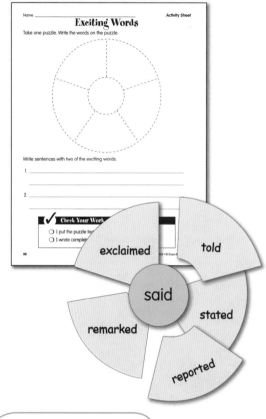

Writing Tips

People use the same words over and over again. These are called overused words.

Writers look in a dictionary or a thesaurus to find more exciting words to use. They exchange the ordinary word for a more exciting word that means about the same thing.

Example

Overused word—said

Mary **said** that she was invited to a party.

More exciting word—exclaimed

Mary **exclaimed** that she was invited to a party.

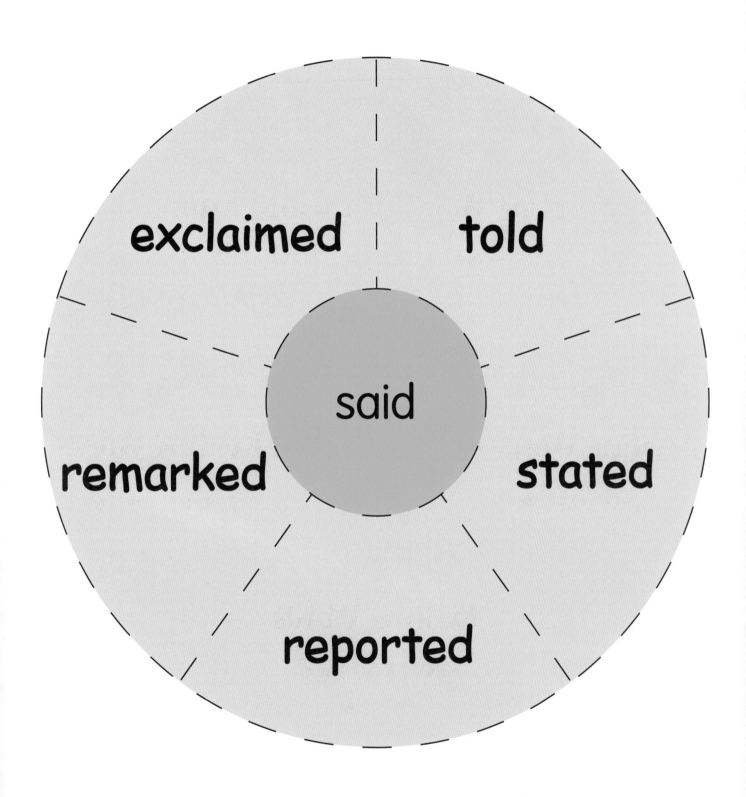

exclaimed

told

said

remarked

stated

reported

Exciting Words

© Evan-Moor Corp. • EMC 6003

Exciting Words

© Evan-Moor Corp. • EMC 6003

Exciting Words

© Evan-Moor Corp. • EMC 6003

Exciting Words

© Evan-Moor Corp.
EMC 6003

Exciting Words

© Evan-Moor Corp. • EMC 6003

Exciting Words

© Evan-Moor Corp. • EMC 6003

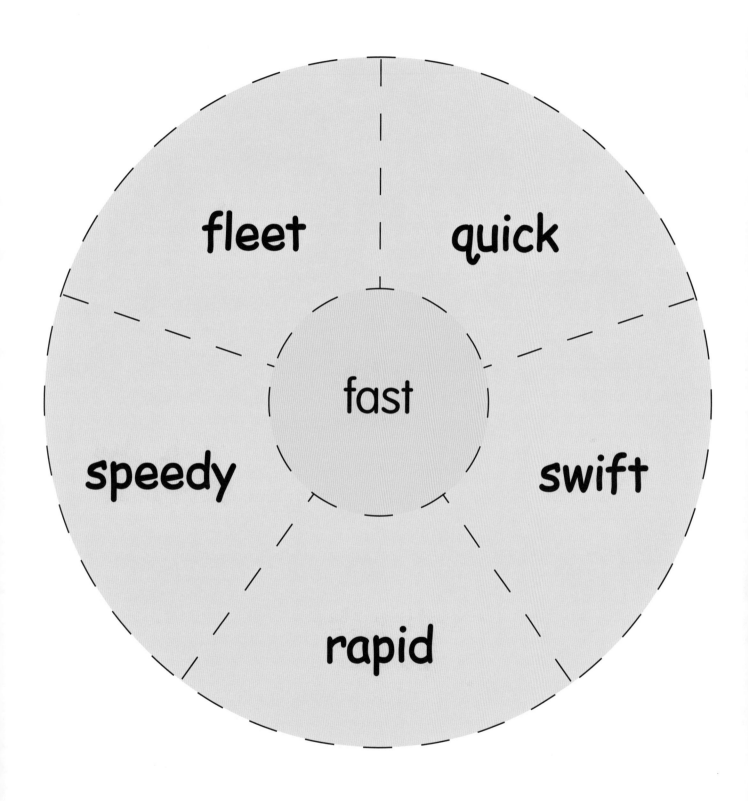

fleet

quick

fast

speedy

swift

rapid

Exciting Words

© Evan-Moor Corp. • EMC 6003

Exciting Words

© Evan-Moor Corp. • EMC 6003

Exciting Words

© Evan-Moor Corp. • EMC 6003

Exciting Words

© Evan-Moor Corp.
EMC 6003

Exciting Words

© Evan-Moor Corp. • EMC 6003

Exciting Words

© Evan-Moor Corp. • EMC 6003

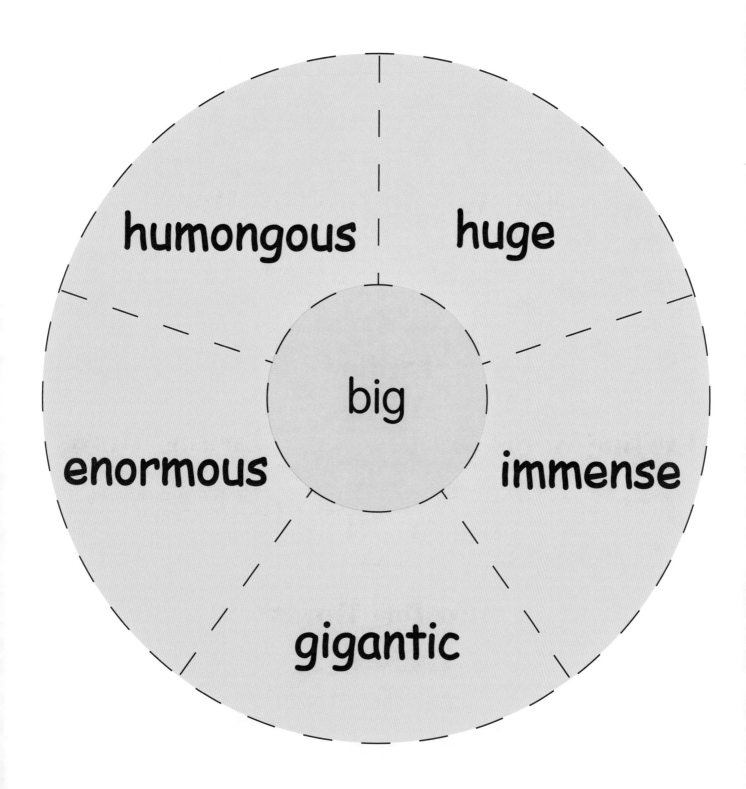

humongous

huge

big

enormous

immense

gigantic

Exciting Words

© Evan-Moor Corp. • EMC 6003

Exciting Words

© Evan-Moor Corp. • EMC 6003

Exciting Words

© Evan-Moor Corp.

EMC 6003

Exciting Words

© Evan-Moor Corp. • EMC 6003

Exciting Words

© Evan-Moor Corp. • EMC 6003

Exciting Words

© Evan-Moor Corp. • EMC 6003

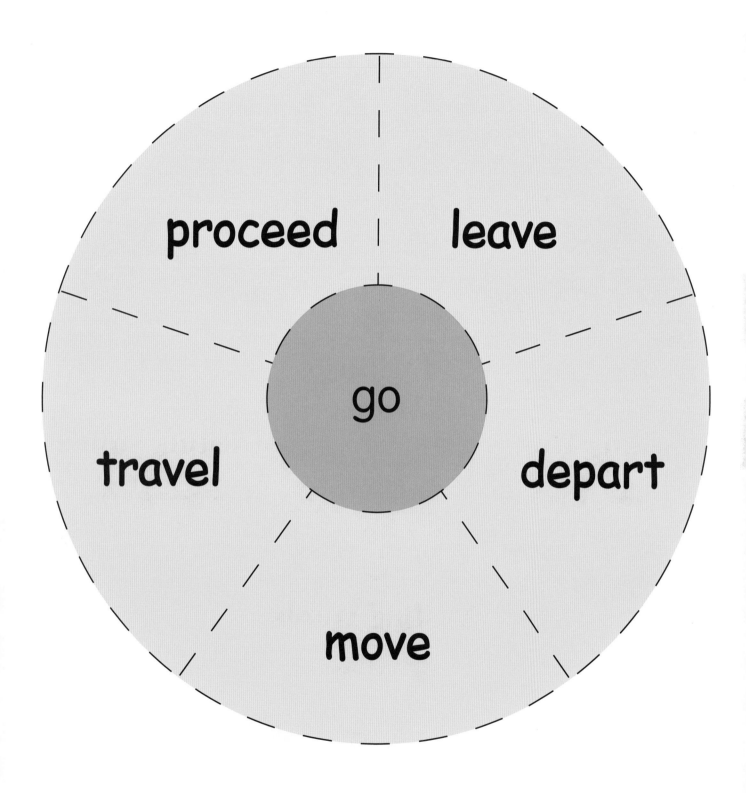

Exciting Words

© Evan-Moor Corp. • EMC 6003

Exciting Words

© Evan-Moor Corp. • EMC 6003

Exciting Words

© Evan-Moor Corp. • EMC 6003

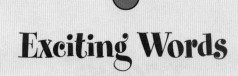

Exciting Words

© Evan-Moor Corp.
EMC 6003

Exciting Words

© Evan-Moor Corp. • EMC 6003

Exciting Words

© Evan-Moor Corp. • EMC 6003

Eight on a List

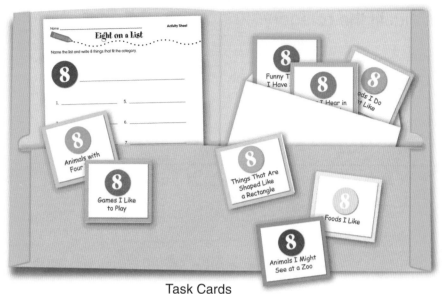

Task Cards

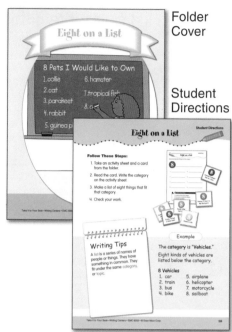

Folder Cover

Student Directions

Preparing the Center

1. Prepare a folder following the directions on page 3.

    Cover—page 113

    Student Directions—page 115

    Task Cards—pages 117 and 119

2. Reproduce a supply of the activity sheet on page 112.

Using the Center

1. The student selects a task card and an activity sheet.

2. The student writes a list of eight things that fit the category. How to write a list is modeled in the student directions.

3. Then the student evaluates the writing task using the checklist on the activity sheet.

Name _____

Eight on a List

Name the list and write 8 things that fit the category.

 _____

1. _____   5. _____

2. _____   6. _____

3. _____   7. _____

4. _____   8. _____

✔ Check Your Work

○ I wrote the name of the category.

○ The words on my list fit the category.

○ I checked my spelling.

Eight on a List

8 Pets I Would Like to Own

1. collie
2. cat
3. parakeet
4. rabbit
5. guinea pig
6. hamster
7. tropical fish
8. c

Eight on a List

Follow These Steps:

1. Take an activity sheet and a card from the folder.

2. Read the card. Write the category on the activity sheet.

3. Make a list of eight things that fit that category.

4. Check your work.

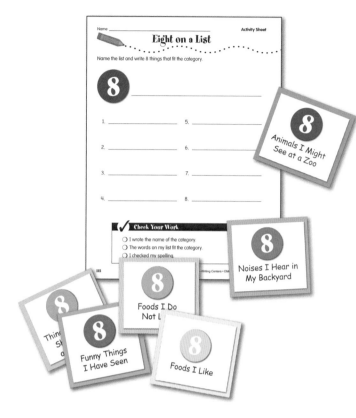

Writing Tips

A list is a series of names of people or things. They have something in common. They fit under the same category, or topic.

Example

The **category** is "**Vehicles**."

Eight kinds of vehicles are listed below the category.

8 Vehicles

1. car
2. train
3. bus
4. bike

5. airplane
6. helicopter
7. motorcycle
8. sailboat

Funny Things I Have Seen

Foods I Do Not Like

Foods I Like

Things That Are Shaped Like a Rectangle

Noises I Hear in My Backyard

Animals I Might See at a Zoo

Eight on a List

Eight on a List

Eight on a List

Eight on a List

Eight on a List

Eight on a List

Games I Like to Play

Animals with Four Legs

Things Smaller Than a Quarter

Things to Do on the Playground

Names of Special People I Know

Presents I Would Like to Receive

Eight on a List

Eight on a List

Eight on a List

Eight on a List

Eight on a List

Eight on a List

Vacation Postcards

Task Cards

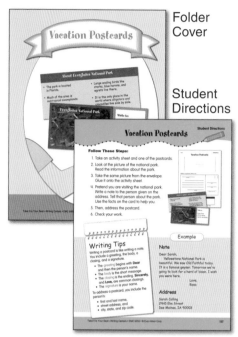

Folder Cover

Student Directions

Preparing the Center

1. Prepare a folder following the directions on page 3.

   Cover—page 125

   Student Directions—page 127

   Postcards—pages 129 and 131

2. Reproduce a supply of the activity sheet on page 122 and the pictures on pages 123 and 124. Cut the pictures apart and place them in an envelope in the folder.

Using the Center

1. The student selects a postcard and an activity sheet. The student looks at the picture and reads the information on the front and back of the card.

2. Next, the student takes the same picture from the envelope and glues it on the activity sheet.

3. Then the student imagines visiting the location and completes the postcard with a note and the address. How to write a postcard is modeled in the student directions.

4. Finally, the student evaluates the writing task using the checklist on the activity sheet.

Vacation Postcards

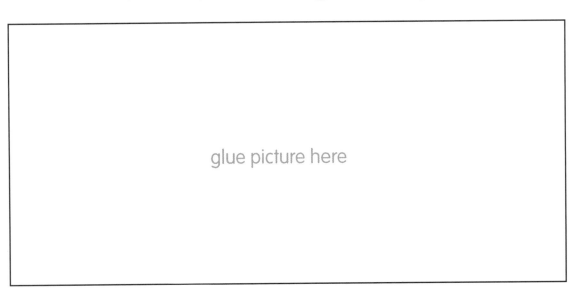

Address the postcard. Write a note.

_____ ,
(greeting)

_____

_____

_____

_____ ,
(closing)

_____
(sign your name)

_____
(name)

_____
(street)

_____
(city, state, zip code)

✔ Check Your Work

◯ I wrote a note.

◯ I signed the note.

◯ I addressed the card.

Denali National Park

Everglades National Park

Grand Canyon National Park

Hawaii Volcanoes National Park

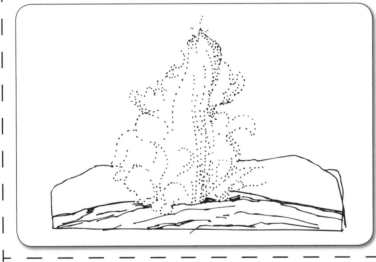

Yellowstone National Park

Yosemite National Park

Vacation Postcards

About Everglades National Park

- The park is located in Florida.

- Much of the area is subtropical swamplands.

- Large wading birds like storks, blue herons, and egrets live there.

- It is the only place in the world where alligators and crocodiles live side by side.

Everglades National Park

© Stefan E

Write to:

Grace Jones
179 4th Street
Seattle, WA 00003

Vacation Postcards

Follow These Steps:

1. Take an activity sheet and one of the postcards.

2. Look at the picture of the national park. Read the information about the park.

3. Take the same picture from the envelope. Glue it onto the activity sheet.

4. Pretend you are visiting the national park. Write a note to the person given on the address. Tell that person about the park. Use the facts on the card to help you.

5. Then, address the postcard.

6. Check your work.

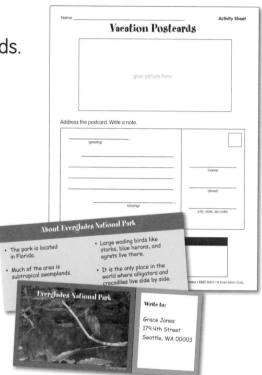

Writing Tips

Writing a postcard is like writing a note. You include a greeting, the body, a closing, and a signature.

- The greeting begins with **Dear** and then the person's name.
- The body is the short message.
- The closing is the ending. **Sincerely,** and **Love,** are common closings.
- The signature is your name.

To address a postcard, you include the person's:

- first and last name,
- street address, and
- city, state, and zip code.

Example

Note

Dear Sarah,
    Yellowstone National Park is beautiful. We saw Old Faithful today. It is a famous geyser. Tomorrow we're going to look for a herd of bison. I wish you were here.
             Love,
             Rosa

Address

Sarah Colling
2945 Elm Street
Des Moines, IA 90003

Denali National Park

© Vera Bogaerts

Write to:

Carlos Gomez
394 South Lake
Austin, TX 00005

Everglades National Park

© Stefan Ekernas

Write to:

Grace Jones
179 4th Street
Seattle, WA 00003

Grand Canyon National Park

© Jason Cheever

Write to:

Jake Young
15 Elm Street
Apex, NC 00001

About Denali National Park

- The park is located in Alaska.

- Large animals like grizzly bears, caribou, and moose live there.

- Mount McKinley is the highest peak in North America.

- Mount McKinley is 20,320 feet high.

About Everglades National Park

- The park is located in Florida.

- Much of the area is subtropical swamplands.

- Large wading birds like storks, blue herons, and egrets live there.

- It is the only place in the world where alligators and crocodiles live side by side.

About Grand Canyon National Park

- The park is located in Arizona.

- The Grand Canyon is 277 miles long and about 1 mile deep.

- The Colorado River flows through the canyon.

- Mules take visitors down into the canyon.

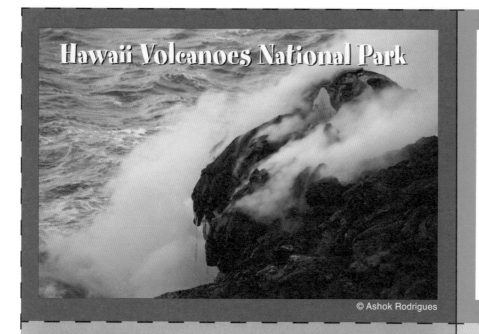

Hawaii Volcanoes National Park

© Ashok Rodrigues

Write to:

Annie Lambert
150 Lake Ave.
Martin, TN 00007

Yellowstone National Park

© Chris Reed

Write to:

Kim Lee
60 Grand Ave.
Dallas, TX 00004

Yosemite National Park

© Steve Schaeffer

Write to:

Maria Toscano
Route 247
Enid, OK 00006

About Hawaii Volcanoes National Park

- The park is located on the Big Island of Hawaii.

- It has the largest volcano in the world—Mauna Loa.

- It has the most active volcano in the world—Kilauea.

- Visitors can see Kilauea erupt from the shoreline at the base of the mountain.

About Yellowstone National Park

- The park is located in Wyoming, Idaho, and Montana.

- Bears, elk, and bison (American buffaloes) roam the park.

- It has more geysers and hot springs than any other place on Earth.

- Old Faithful is the most famous geyser. It erupts about every 76 minutes.

About Yosemite National Park

- The park is located in California.

- It is in the Sierra Nevada Mountains.

- Upper and Lower Yosemite Falls are among the 10 highest waterfalls in North America.

- Rock climbers like to go up Half Dome and El Capitan, which are steep granite rock masses.

 Take It to Your Seat—Writing Centers • EMC 6003 • © Evan-Moor Corp.

Story Starters

Story Starter Cards

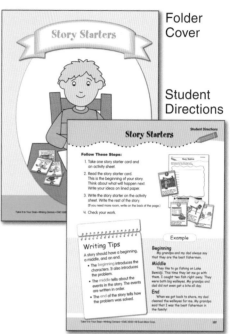

Folder Cover

Student Directions

Preparing the Center

1. Prepare a folder following the directions on page 3.

   Cover—page 135

   Student Directions—page 137

   Story Starter Cards—pages 139–143

2. Reproduce a supply of the activity sheet on page 134. Provide a supply of lined paper.

Using the Center

1. The student takes the story starter cards and an activity sheet.

2. The student chooses a card. The student writes down ideas for the rest of the story.

3. Next, the student copies the story starter onto the activity page.

4. Then the student writes the rest of the story. How to write a story is modeled in the student directions.

5. Finally, the student evaluates the writing task using the checklist on the activity sheet.

Name _____

Story Starters

Write the story starter. Then, finish writing the story.
If you need more room, write on the back of the page.

_____

_____

_____

_____

_____

_____

_____

_____

_____

_____

✔ Check Your Work

◯ I wrote a story that had a beginning, a middle, and an end.

◯ I wrote complete sentences.

Story Starters

Story Starters

Follow These Steps:

1. Take one story starter card and an activity sheet.

2. Read the story starter card. This is the beginning of your story. Think about what will happen next. Write your ideas on lined paper.

3. Write the story starter on the activity sheet. Write the rest of the story.

   (If you need more room, write on the back of the page.)

4. Check your work.

Writing Tips

A story should have a beginning, a middle, and an end.

- The beginning introduces the characters. It also introduces the problem.

- The middle tells about the events in the story. The events are written in order.

- The end of the story tells how the problem was solved.

Example

Beginning

My grandpa and my dad always say that they are the best fishermen.

Middle

They like to go fishing on Lake Bemidji. This time they let me go with them. I caught two fish right away. They were both big walleyes. My grandpa and dad did not even get a bite all day.

End

When we got back to shore, my dad cleaned the walleyes for me. My grandpa said that I was the best fisherman in the family!

138

1

The sign said "KEEP OUT!" I just had to find out what was behind that gate!

2

Suzanne could not believe her eyes! Harry the hamster was gone!

3

All the kids were singing "Happy Birthday" to Christopher. That's when Sparky joined in the fun.

4

Joseph loved riding his new bike in the park.

Story Starters

Story Starters

Story Starters

Story Starters

5

At recess, Olivia watched her friends. They looked like they were having so much fun.

6

This was the big day. Ashanti had never ridden a pony before.

7

The forest was on fire! The rescue helicopter was ready to land.

8

Rover and Princess were the best of friends. But they were always getting into trouble.

Story Starters

Story Starters

Story Starters

Story Starters

9

Mother opened Nadia's bedroom door. She was surprised to see that the girls were still awake.

10

Jamal was at bat. He had three balls and two strikes.

11

Jake and Molly begged their parents. They really wanted to ride the Scream Machine.

12

One day, Leon was digging for worms. He pulled a box out of the hole.

Story Starters

Story Starters

Story Starters

Story Starters

A Friendly Letter

Task Cards

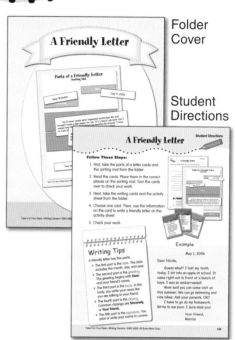

Folder Cover

Student Directions

Preparing the Center

1. Prepare a folder following the directions on page 3.

   Cover—page 147

   Student Directions—page 149

   Sorting Mat—page 151

   Parts of a Letter Cards—page 153

   Task Cards—pages 155 and 157

2. Reproduce a supply of the activity sheet on page 146.

Using the Center

1. The student takes the parts of a letter cards and the sorting mat from the folder.

2. Next, the student places the five parts of a friendly letter in the correct places on the sorting mat. The cards are self-checking.

3. Then the student takes the task cards and the activity sheet from the folder.

4. The student chooses one task card to use to write a friendly letter on the activity sheet. How to write a friendly letter is modeled in the student directions.

5. Finally, the student evaluates the writing task using the checklist on the activity sheet.

A Friendly Letter

Choose a card. Use the information on the card to write a friendly letter.

_____

_____

_____

_____

_____

_____

_____

_____

_____

_____

✓ Check Your Work

○ I wrote the date and a greeting.

○ I wrote the body of the letter.

○ I wrote a closing and signed the letter.

A Friendly Letter

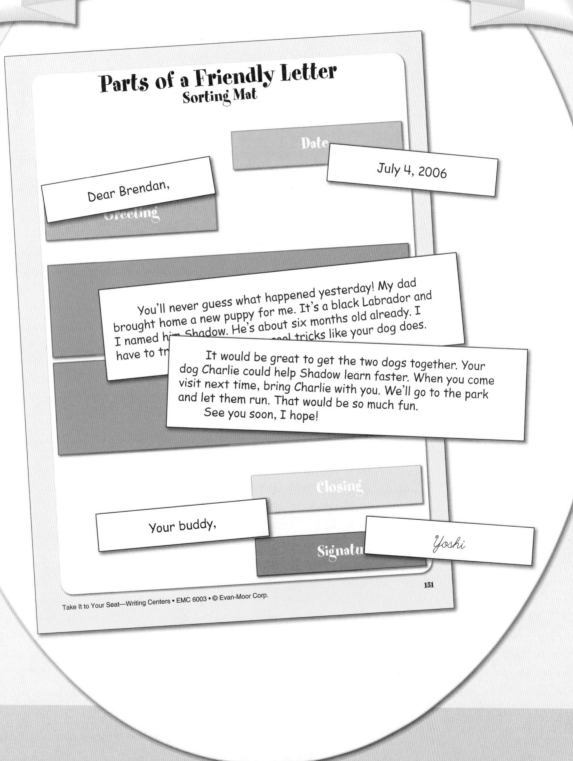

Parts of a Friendly Letter
Sorting Mat

Date

July 4, 2006

Dear Brendan,

Greeting

You'll never guess what happened yesterday! My dad brought home a new puppy for me. It's a black Labrador and I named him Shadow. He's about six months old already. I have to tr... cool tricks like your dog does.

It would be great to get the two dogs together. Your dog Charlie could help Shadow learn faster. When you come visit next time, bring Charlie with you. We'll go to the park and let them run. That would be so much fun.
See you soon, I hope!

Closing

Your buddy,

Signature

Yoshi

151

Take It to Your Seat—Writing Centers • EMC 6003 • © Evan-Moor Corp.

A Friendly Letter

Follow These Steps:

1. First, take the parts of a letter cards and the sorting mat from the folder.

2. Read the cards. Place them in the correct places on the sorting mat. Turn the cards over to check your work.

3. Next, take the writing cards and the activity sheet from the folder.

4. Choose one card. Then, use the information on the card to write a friendly letter on the activity sheet.

5. Check your work.

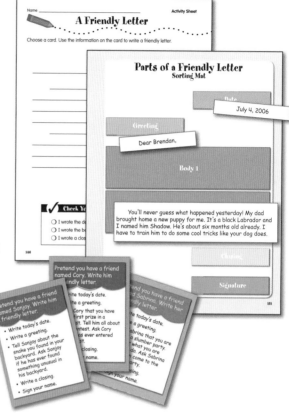

Writing Tips

A friendly letter has five parts:

- The first part is the date. The date includes the month, day, and year.
- The second part is the greeting. The greeting begins with **Dear** and your friend's name.
- The third part is the body. In the body, you write your news like you are talking to your friend.
- The fourth part is the closing. Common closings are **Sincerely,** or **Your friend,**.
- The fifth part is the signature. You print or write your name in cursive.

Example

May 1, 2006

Dear Nicole,

Guess what? I lost my tooth today. I bit into an apple at school. It came right out in front of a bunch of boys. I was so embarrassed!

Mom said you can come visit us this summer. We can go swimming and ride bikes. Ask your parents. OK?

I have to go do my homework. Write to me soon. I sure miss you!

Your friend,
Marcia

Parts of a Friendly Letter
Sorting Mat

Date

Greeting

Body 1

Body 2

Closing

Signature

July 4, 2006

Dear Brendan,

Your buddy,

Yoshi

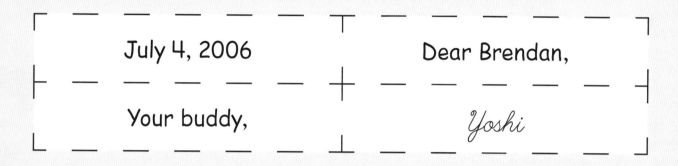

You'll never guess what happened yesterday! My dad brought home a new puppy for me. It's a black Labrador and I named him Shadow. He's about six months old already. I have to train him to do some cool tricks like your dog does.

It would be great to get the two dogs together. Your dog Charlie could help Shadow learn faster. When you come visit next time, bring Charlie with you. We'll go to the park and let them run. That would be so much fun.
See you soon, I hope!

Greeting

A Friendly Letter
© Evan-Moor Corp. • EMC 6003

Date

A Friendly Letter
© Evan-Moor Corp. • EMC 6003

Signature

A Friendly Letter
© Evan-Moor Corp. • EMC 6003

Closing

A Friendly Letter
© Evan-Moor Corp. • EMC 6003

Body 1

A Friendly Letter

© Evan-Moor Corp. • EMC 6003

Body 2

A Friendly Letter

© Evan-Moor Corp. • EMC 6003

Pretend you have a friend named Alejandro. Write him a friendly letter.

- Write today's date.
- Write a greeting.
- Tell Alejandro about the new bike you got for your birthday. Ask Alejandro to come over to ride bikes with you.
- Write a closing.
- Sign your name.

Pretend you have a friend named Kimberly. Write her a friendly letter.

- Write today's date.
- Write a greeting.
- Tell Kimberly that you have moved into a new house. Tell her what it's like. Ask Kimberly to visit your new house.
- Write a closing.
- Sign your name.

Pretend you have a friend named Jonathon. Write him a friendly letter.

- Write today's date.
- Write a greeting.
- Tell Jonathon that you are going to summer camp. Tell him what the camp is about. Ask Jonathon if he is going to summer camp.
- Write a closing.
- Sign your name.

Pretend you have a friend named Tanya. Write her a friendly letter.

- Write today's date.
- Write a greeting.
- Tell Tanya that you are trying out for the soccer team. Tell her about playing soccer at school. Ask Tanya what sports she likes to play.
- Write a closing.
- Sign your name.

A Friendly Letter

A Friendly Letter

A Friendly Letter

A Friendly Letter

Pretend you have a friend named Sonjay. Write him a friendly letter.

- Write today's date.
- Write a greeting.
- Tell Sonjay about the snake you found in your backyard. Ask Sonjay if he has ever found something unusual in his backyard.
- Write a closing.
- Sign your name.

Pretend you have a friend named Tamara. Write her a friendly letter.

- Write today's date.
- Write a greeting.
- Tell Tamara that you are moving to another state. Tell her what is good about it. Tell her what part makes you sad. Ask Tamara to come visit you in your new home.
- Write a closing.
- Sign your name.

Pretend you have a friend named Cory. Write him a friendly letter.

- Write today's date.
- Write a greeting.
- Tell Cory that you have won first prize in a contest. Tell him all about the contest. Ask Cory if he has ever entered a contest.
- Write a closing.
- Sign your name.

Pretend you have a friend named Sabrina. Write her a friendly letter.

- Write today's date.
- Write a greeting.
- Tell Sabrina that you are having a slumber party. Tell her what you are going to do. Ask Sabrina if she can come to the slumber party.
- Write a closing.
- Sign your name.

A Friendly Letter

A Friendly Letter

A Friendly Letter

A Friendly Letter

Checking for Errors

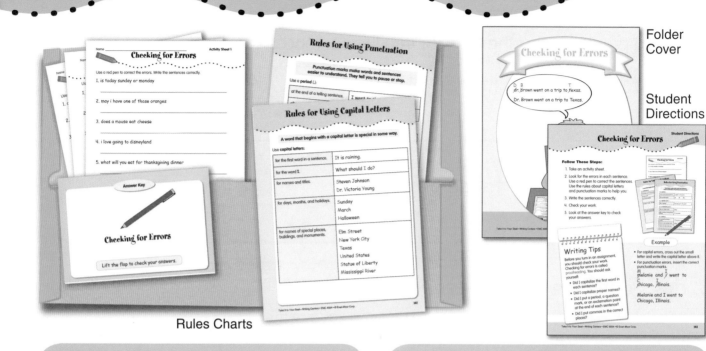

Folder Cover

Student Directions

Rules Charts

Preparing the Center

1. Prepare a folder following the directions on page 3.

   Cover—page 163

   Student Directions—page 165

   Rules Charts—pages 167 and 169

   Answer Key—pages 171 and 172

2. Reproduce a supply of the activity sheets on pages 160–162. Provide red pens for student use.

Using the Center

1. The student selects an activity sheet. The rules charts are provided as a resource if the student needs help. *Note: The teacher may want to choose which activity sheet the student needs to do for practice.*

2. Next, the student uses a red pen to mark corrections for each sentence on the activity sheet. How to check for errors is modeled in the student directions.

3. Then the student copies each sentence correctly.

4. The student evaluates the editing and writing task using the checklist on each activity sheet.

5. Finally, the student checks the answers using the answer key.

Checking for Errors

Use a red pen to correct the errors. Write the sentences correctly.

1. is today sunday or monday

   _____

2. may i have one of those oranges

   _____

3. does a mouse eat cheese

   _____

4. i love going to disneyland

   _____

5. what will you eat for thanksgiving dinner

   _____

   _____

6. doug was born on may 7 1997

   _____

✓ Check Your Work

◯ I used capital letters correctly.

◯ I used punctuation marks correctly.

◯ I wrote the sentences correctly.

 Take It to Your Seat—Writing Centers • EMC 6003 • © Evan-Moor Corp.

Name _____

Checking for Errors

Use a red pen to correct the errors. Write the sentences correctly.

1. i can't believe you like spinach

_____

2. carlos sailed on the pacific ocean

_____

3. watch out for the ball

_____

4. will you play with me

_____

5. today is friday may 21

_____

6. did you climb windom peak

_____

✔ Check Your Work

○ I used capital letters correctly.

○ I used punctuation marks correctly.

○ I wrote the sentences correctly.

Checking for Errors

Use a red pen to correct the errors. Write the sentences correctly.

1. does mr jones live in oregon

_____

2. that's a great idea

_____

3. will you help jim tom and me clean up the mess

_____

_____

4. her birthday is on easter sunday this year

_____

_____

5. mrs martin visited england

_____

6. did you see bears monkeys and kangaroos at the zoo

_____

_____

✓ Check Your Work

○ I used capital letters correctly.

○ I used punctuation marks correctly.

○ I wrote the sentences correctly.

Checking for Errors

Checking for Errors

Follow These Steps:

1. Take an activity sheet.

2. Look for the errors in each sentence. Use a red pen to correct the sentences. Use the rules about capital letters and punctuation marks to help you.

3. Write the sentences correctly.

4. Check your work.

5. Look at the answer key to check your answers.

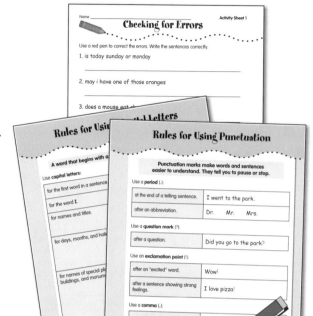

Writing Tips

Before you turn in an assignment, you should check your work. Checking for errors is called proofreading. You should ask yourself:

- Did I capitalize the first word in each sentence?

- Did I capitalize proper names?

- Did I put a period, a question mark, or an exclamation point at the end of each sentence?

- Did I put commas in the correct places?

Example

- For capital errors, cross out the small letter and write the capital letter above it.

- For punctuation errors, insert the correct punctuation marks.

melanie and i went to
chicago, illinois.

Melanie and I went to
Chicago, Illinois.

Rules for Using Capital Letters

A word that begins with a capital letter is special in some way.

Use **capital letters:**

for the first word in a sentence.	It is raining.
for the word **I**.	What should I do?
for names and titles.	Steven Johnson Dr. Victoria Young
for days, months, and holidays.	Sunday March Halloween
for names of special places, buildings, and monuments.	Elm Street New York City Texas United States Statue of Liberty Mississippi River

168

Rules for Using Punctuation

Punctuation marks make words and sentences easier to understand. They tell you to pause or stop.

Use a **period** (.):

at the end of a telling sentence.	I went to the park.
after an abbreviation.	Dr. Mr. Mrs.

Use a **question mark** (?):

after a question.	Did you go to the park?

Use an **exclamation point** (!):

after an "excited" word.	Wow!
after a sentence showing strong feelings.	I love pizza!

Use a **comma** (,):

to separate three things in a series.	I like pizza, popcorn, and pie.
between a city and state name.	Dallas, Texas
between the day and the year.	March 14, 2006

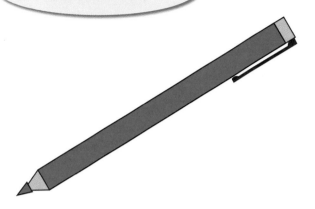

Checking for Errors

Lift the flap to check your answers.

Activity Sheet 1
Answer Key

1. I̶s today S̶unday or M̶onday?   Is today Sunday or Monday?

2. M̶ay I̶ have one of those oranges?   May I have one of those oranges?

3. D̶oes a mouse eat cheese?   Does a mouse eat cheese?

4. I̶ love going to D̶isneyland!   I love going to Disneyland!

5. W̶hat will you eat for   What will you eat for

   T̶hanksgiving dinner?   Thanksgiving dinner?

6. D̶oug was born on M̶ay 7, 1997.   Doug was born on May 7, 1997.

Activity Sheet 2
Answer Key

1. I̶ can't believe you like spinach!   I can't believe you like spinach!
    - *I*

2. C̶arlos sailed on the p̶acific o̶cean.   Carlos sailed on the Pacific Ocean.
    - *C*   *P*   *O*

3. W̶atch out for the ball!   Watch out for the ball!
    - *W*

4. W̶ill you play with me?   Will you play with me?
    - *W*

5. T̶oday is F̶riday, M̶ay 21.   Today is Friday, May 21.
    - *T*   *F*   *M*

6. D̶id you climb W̶indom P̶eak?   Did you climb Windom Peak?
    - *D*   *W*   *P*

Activity Sheet 3
Answer Key

1. D̶oes M̶r. J̶ones live in O̶regon?   Does Mr. Jones live in Oregon?
    - *D*   *M J*   *O*

2. T̶hat's a great idea!   That's a great idea!
    - *T*

3. W̶ill you help J̶im, T̶om, and   Will you help Jim, Tom, and
    - *W*   *J*   *T*
   me clean up the mess?   me clean up the mess?

4. H̶er birthday is on E̶aster   Her birthday is on Easter
    - *H*   *E*
   S̶unday this year.   Sunday this year.
    - *S*

5. M̶rs. M̶artin visited E̶ngland.   Mrs. Martin visited England.
    - *M*   *M*   *E*

6. D̶id you see bears, monkeys,   Did you see bears, monkeys,
    - *D*
   and kangaroos at the zoo?   and kangaroos at the zoo?

How Do You Do It?

Task Cards

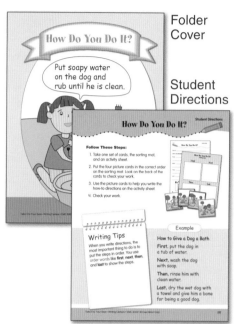

Folder Cover

Student Directions

Preparing the Center

1. Prepare a folder following the directions on page 3.

    Cover—page 175

    Student Directions—page 177

    Sorting Mat—page 179

    Task Cards—pages 181–191

2. Reproduce a supply of the activity sheet on page 174.

Using the Center

1. The student selects one set of task cards, the sorting mat, and an activity sheet.

2. Next, the student puts the four cards in the correct sequence on the sorting mat. The cards are self-checking.

3. Then the student writes the directions for the task, following the sequence of *First, Next, Then,* and *Last.* How to write directions is modeled in the student directions.

4. Finally, the student evaluates the writing task using the checklist on the activity sheet.

Name _____

How Do You Do It?

How to _____

Write the directions.

First, _____

_____

Next, _____

_____

Then, _____

_____

Last, _____

_____

✓ Check Your Work

○ My steps are in the correct order.
○ I wrote complete sentences.
○ I used capital letters correctly.
○ I used punctuation marks correctly.

How Do You Do It?

176

How Do You Do It?

Follow These Steps:

1. Take one set of cards, the sorting mat, and an activity sheet.

2. Put the four picture cards in the correct order on the sorting mat. Look on the back of the cards to check your work.

3. Use the picture cards to help you write the how-to directions on the activity sheet.

4. Check your work.

Writing Tips

When you write directions, the most important thing to do is to put the steps in order. You use order words like **first**, **next**, **then**, and **last** to show the steps.

Example

How to Give a Dog a Bath

First, put the dog in a tub of water.

Next, wash the dog with soap.

Then, rinse him with clean water.

Last, dry the wet dog with a towel and give him a bone for being a good dog.

178

Take It to Your Seat—Writing Centers • EMC 6003 • © Evan-Moor Corp.

How Do You Do It?
Sorting Mat

First

Next

Then

Last

180

How to Brush Your Teeth

Set 1

Next

How Do You Do It?

How to Brush Your Teeth

Set 1

First

How Do You Do It?

How to Brush Your Teeth

Set 1

Last

How Do You Do It?

How to Brush Your Teeth

Set 1

Then

How Do You Do It?

How to Make a Peanut Butter
and Jelly Sandwich

Set 2

Next

How Do You Do It?

How to Make a Peanut Butter
and Jelly Sandwich

Set 2

First

How Do You Do It?

How to Make a Peanut Butter
and Jelly Sandwich

Set 2

Last

How Do You Do It?

How to Make a Peanut Butter
and Jelly Sandwich

Set 2

Then

How Do You Do It?

How to Send a Letter

Set 3

Next

How Do You Do It?

How to Send a Letter

Set 3

First

How Do You Do It?

How to Send a Letter

Set 3

Last

How Do You Do It?

How to Send a Letter

Set 3

Then

How Do You Do It?

How to Give a Dog a Bath

Set 4

Next

How Do You Do It?

How to Give a Dog a Bath

Set 4

First

How Do You Do It?

How to Give a Dog a Bath

Set 4

Last

How Do You Do It?

How to Give a Dog a Bath

Set 4

Then

How Do You Do It?

How to Make a Sundae

Set 5

Next

How Do You Do It?

How to Make a Sundae

Set 5

First

How Do You Do It?

How to Make a Sundae

Set 5

Last

How Do You Do It?

How to Make a Sundae

Set 5

Then

How Do You Do It?

How to Make a Phone Call

Set 6

Next

How Do You Do It?

How to Make a Phone Call

Set 6

First

How Do You Do It?

How to Make a Phone Call

Set 6

Last

How Do You Do It?

How to Make a Phone Call

Set 6

Then

How Do You Do It?